Lina Ng

© RHYTHM MP SDN. BHD.1985
Revised Edition 1995
New Edition: 2001

Published by
RHYTHM MP SDN. BHD.
1947, Lorong IKS Bukit Minyak 2,
Taman IKS Bukit Minyak, 14100 Simpang Ampat,
Penang, Malaysia.
Tel: +60 4 5050246 (Direct Line), +60 4 5073690 (Hunting Line)
Fax: +60 4 5050691
E-mail: rhythmmp@mphsb.com
Website: www.rhythmmp.com

Cover Design by **LIM WAI FUN**

ISBN 967-985-441-8
Order No.: MPM-3002-01

Photocopying Prohibited.
All rights reserved.
Unauthorised reproduction of any part of this publication by any means
including photocopying is an infringement of copyright.

CONTENTS

My

Page	Title
03	Treble & bass
04	Number of counts
05	Game - Balloons For Sale
06	Time signatures
08	Keyboard
09	Notes in the treble
14	Game - Going Carrots
16	Notes in the bass
23	Rests
25	Game - Find The Partners
29	Accidentals
31	Game - At The Baby-Sitters
33	Position of stems
35	Time signatures
36	Game - Fishing
37	Complete bars with notes
38	Complete bars with rests
39	Test

My

TREBLE & BASS

3

Treble Clef / G Clef (**Cuts the G-line**)

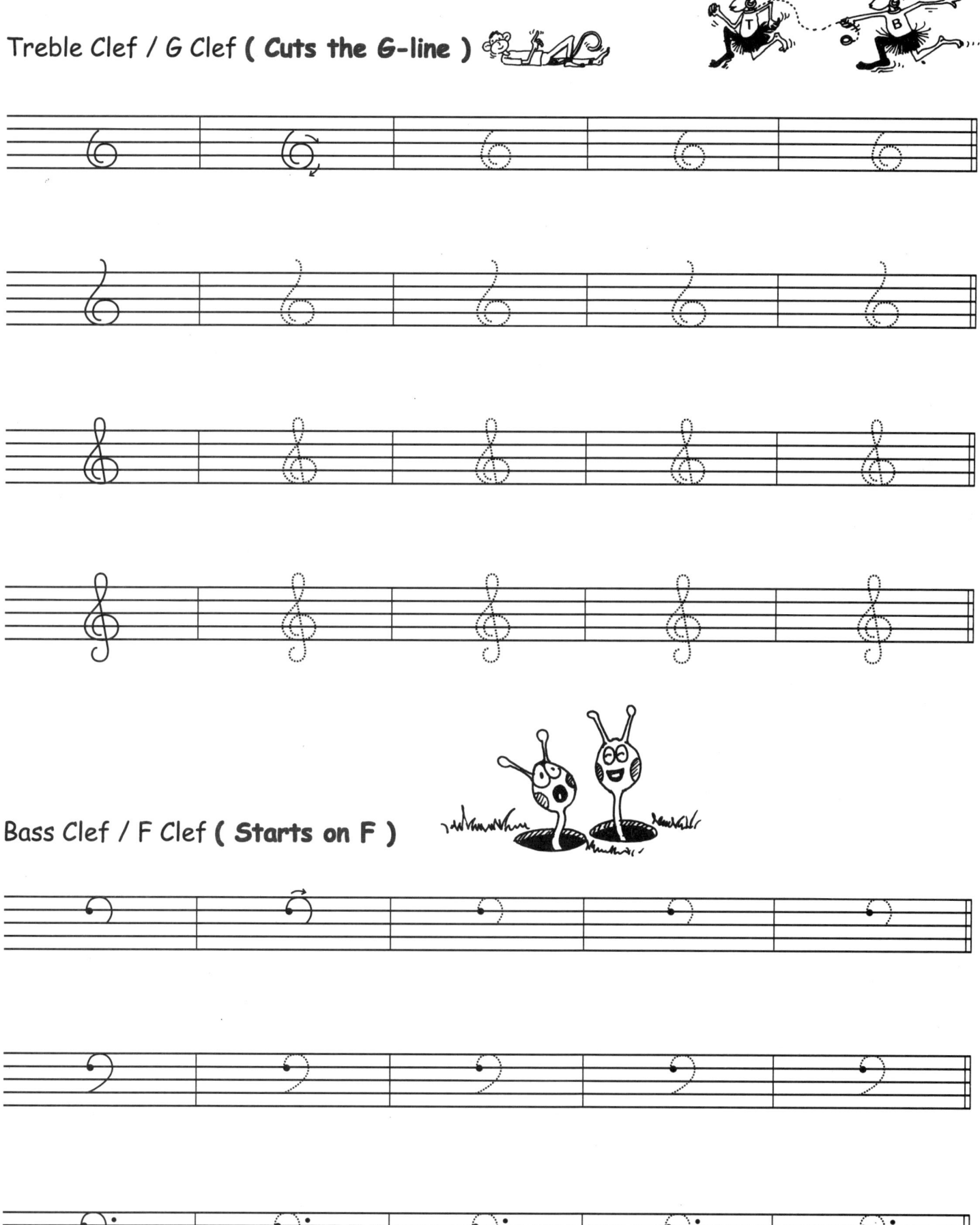

Bass Clef / F Clef (**Starts on F**)

NUMBER OF COUNTS

Semibreve

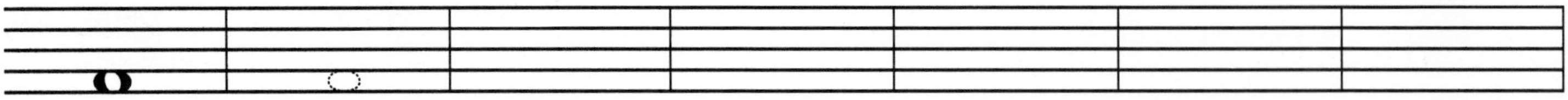

o   4

Dotted Minim

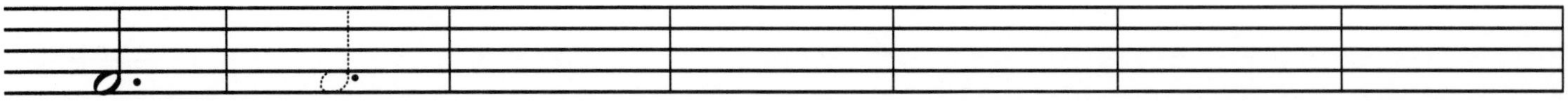

o.   3

Minim

o   2

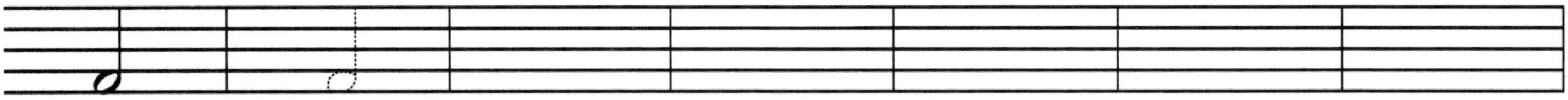

Crotchet

•   1

Write the number of counts.

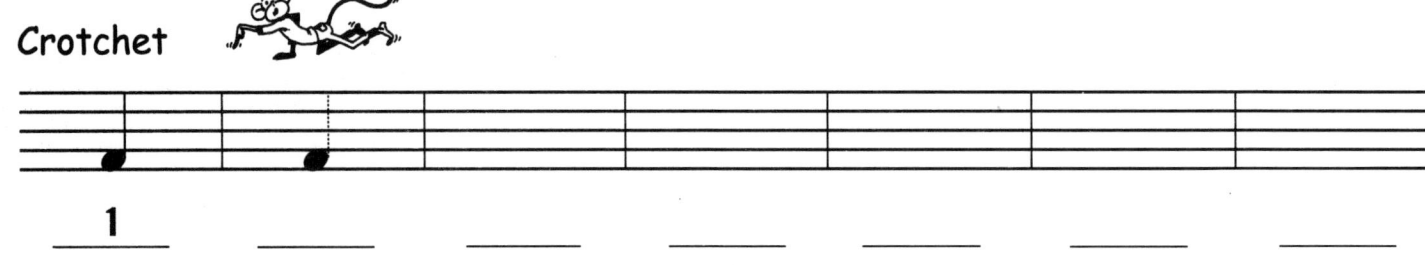

o — 4, d. — ___, d — ___, ♩ — ___, d. — ___, o — ___, ♩ — ___, d — ___

d — ___, o — ___, ♩ — ___, o — ___, d. — ___, ♩ — ___, d — ___, d. — ___

BALLOONS FOR SALE

5

Colour the balloons accordingly.

NO. OF COUNTS	COLOUR
1	RED
2	BLUE
3	YELLOW
4	GREEN

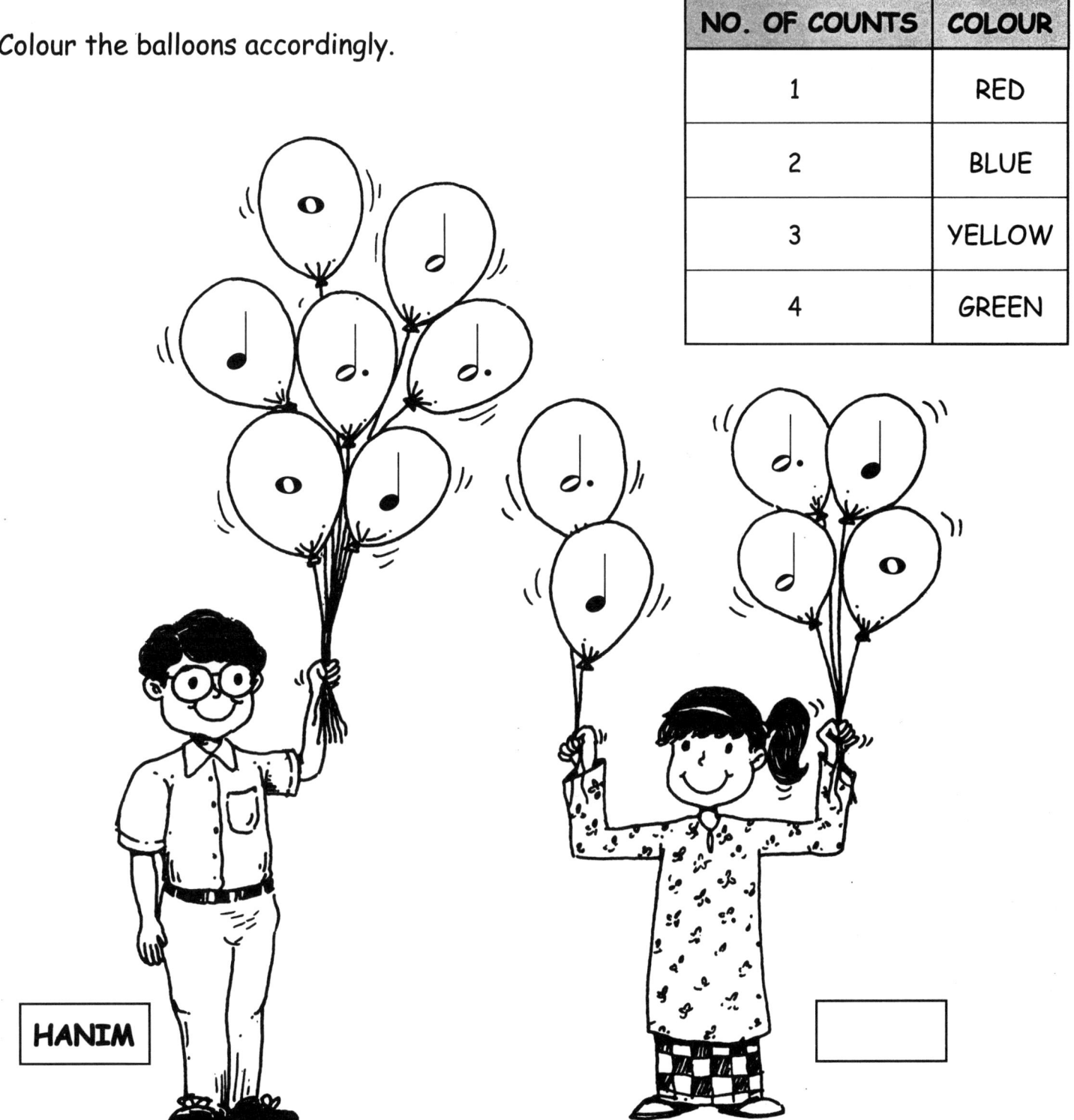

HANIM

Oh-oh, Hanim has one extra balloon. What is the colour of that balloon?
____ ____ ____ ____ ____

Spell Hanim's name from right to left to find out his sister's name.
____ ____ ____ ____ ____

Time Signatures

$\frac{2}{4}$	2 crotchet beats in a bar
$\frac{3}{4}$	3 crotchet beats in a bar
$\frac{4}{4}$	4 crotchet beats in a bar

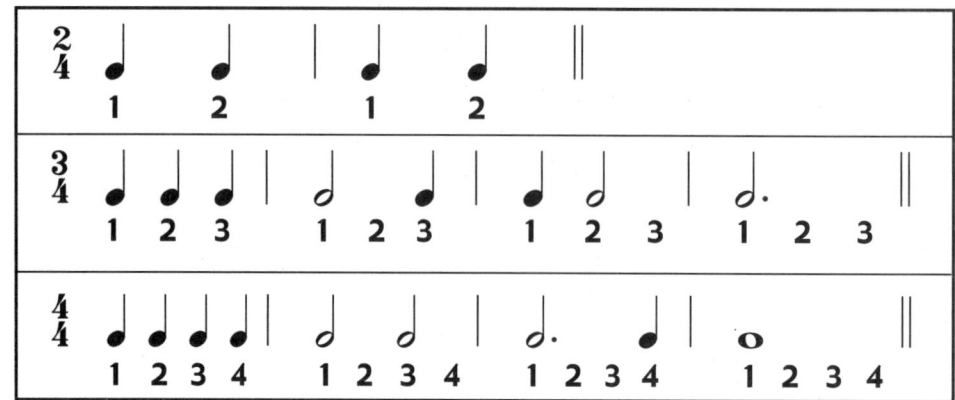

Help the space ship find the places that they may land.
Match as shown.

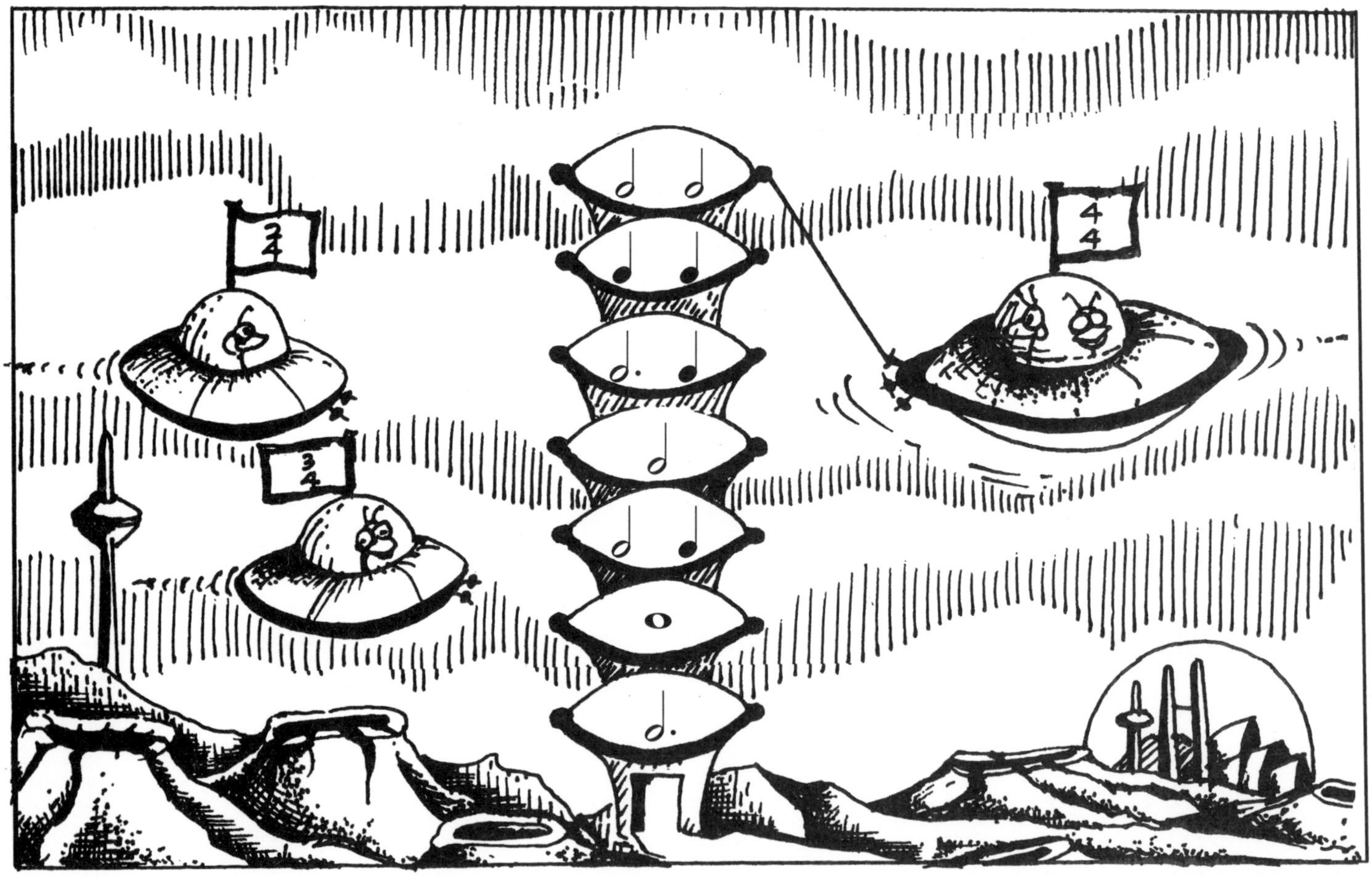

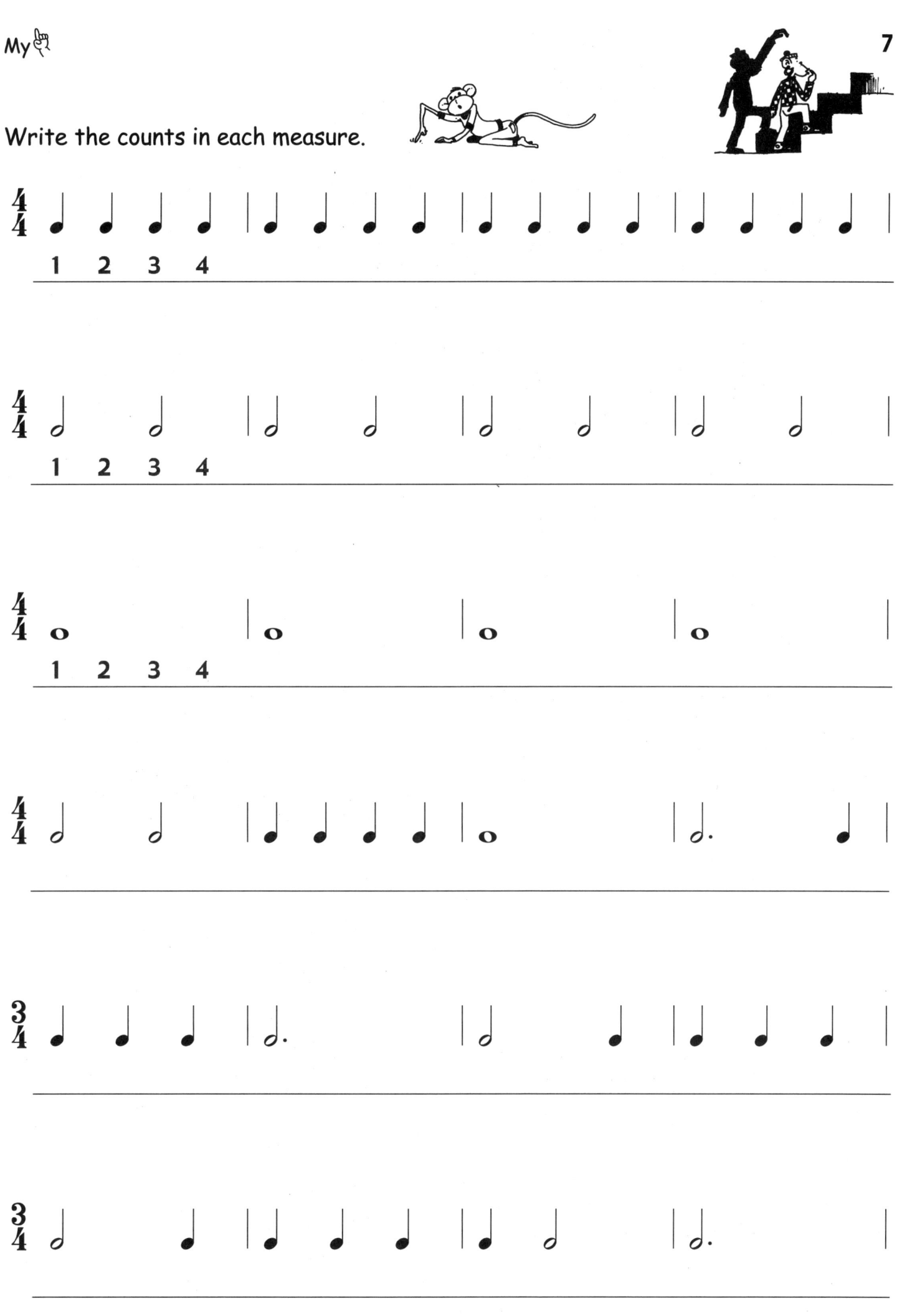

8  My

Print the letter-names on the white keys - C D E F G A B C D E

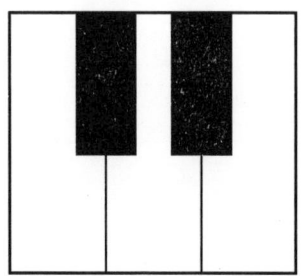 Print the letter-names on the white keys

 Print the letter names on the white keys

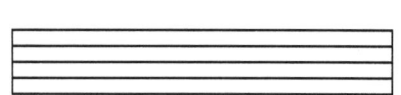

The stave consists of 5 lines

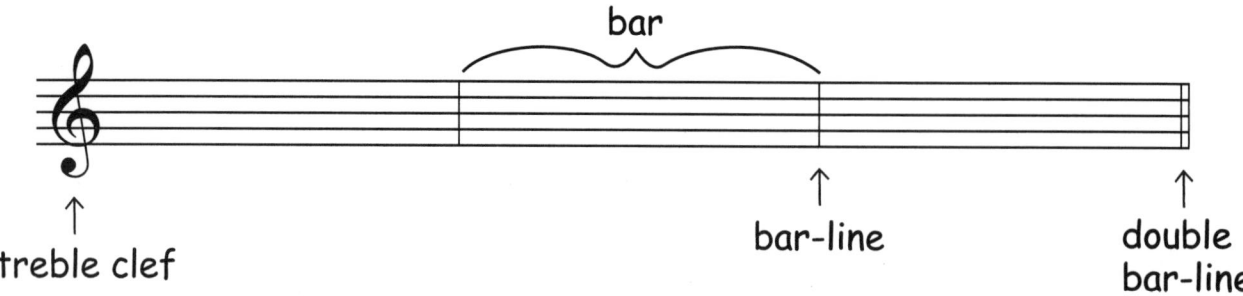

bar

↑ treble clef   ↑ bar-line   ↑ double bar-line

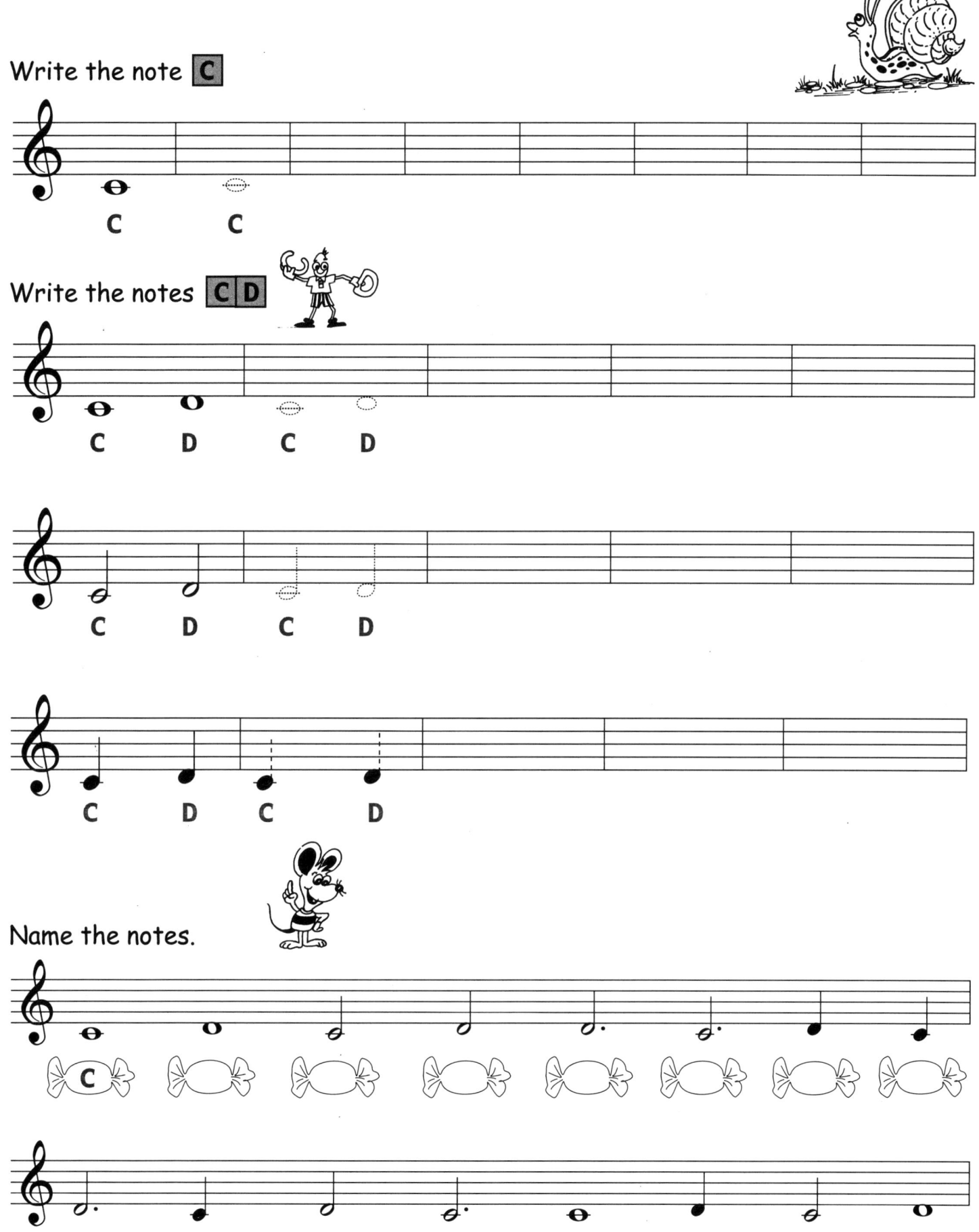

10 My

Write the notes C D E

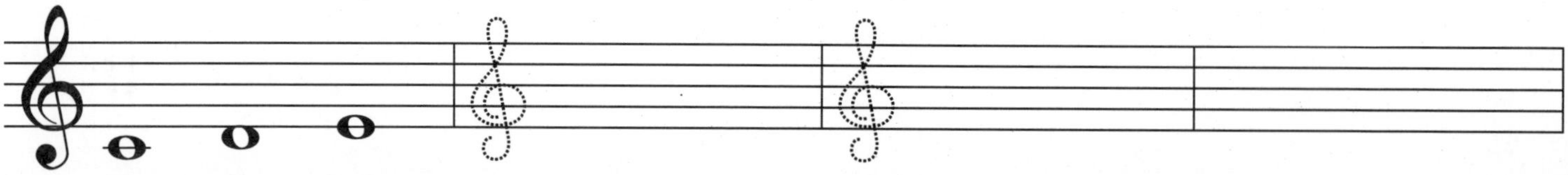

C D E

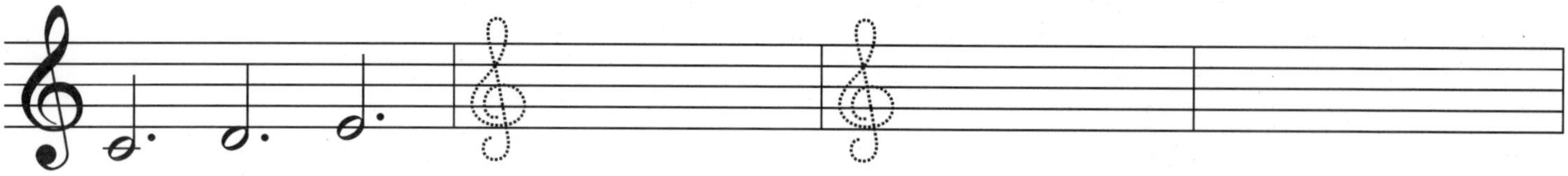

C D E

Name the notes.

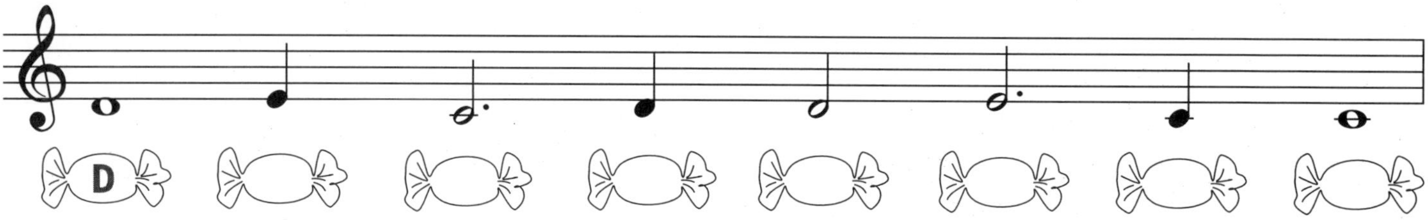

D

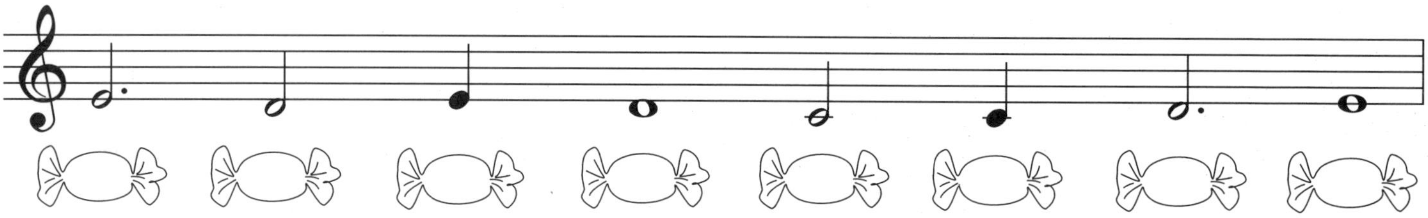

Write the notes.

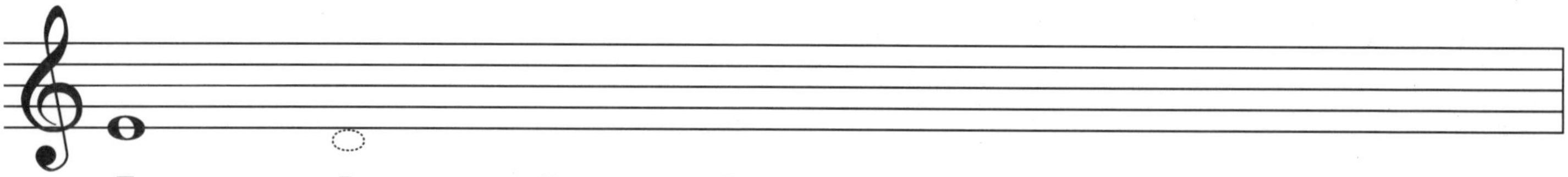

E D C D E D C E

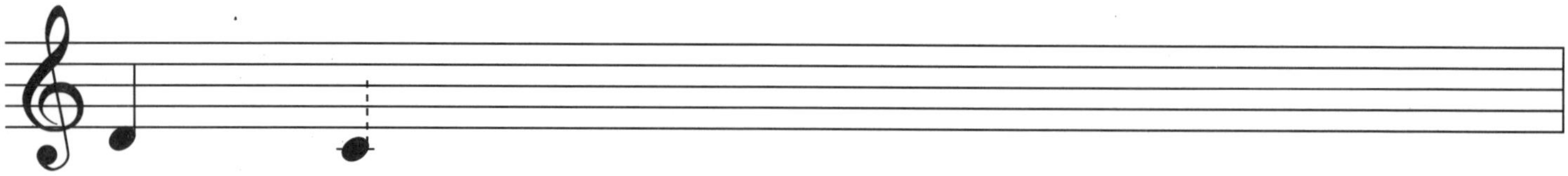

D C E D D C E E

My

11

Match the notes to the correct alphabets.

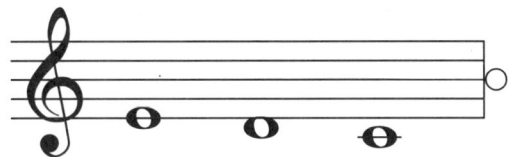
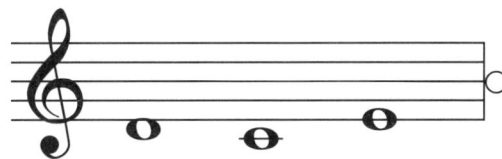
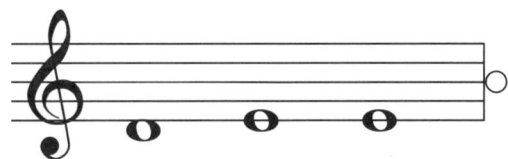
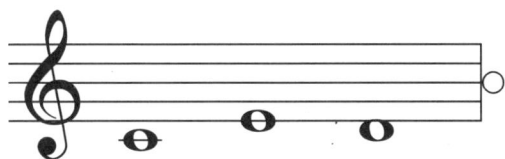
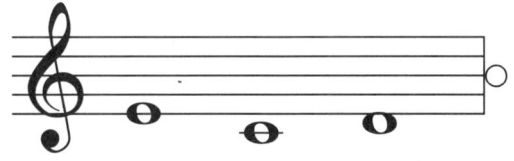
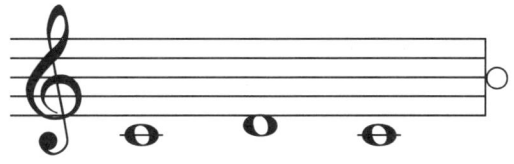
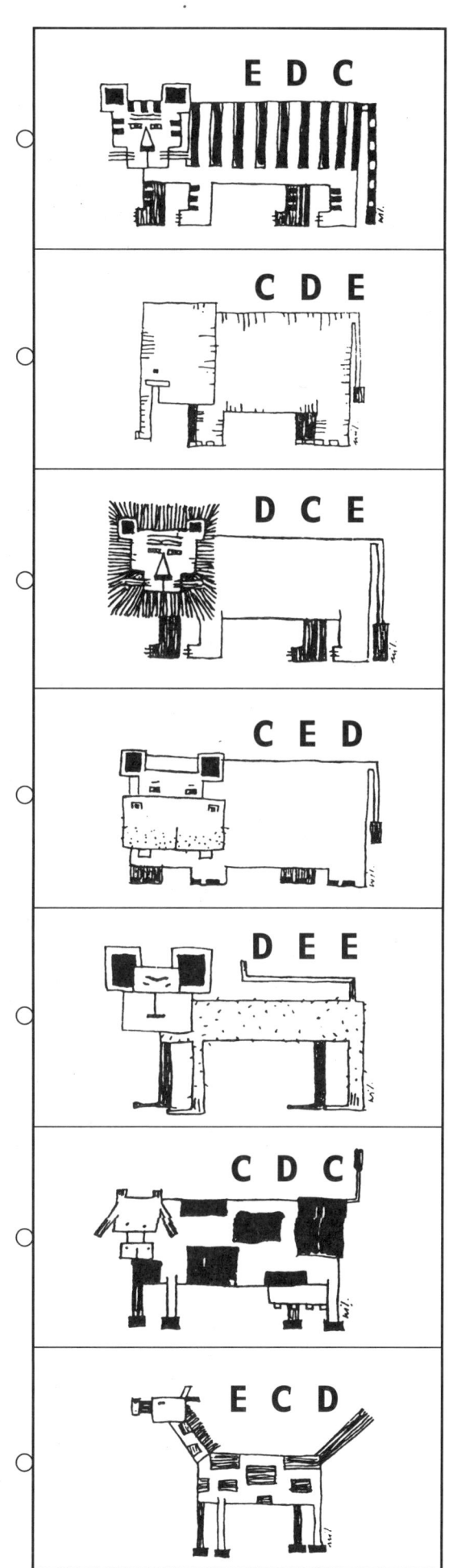

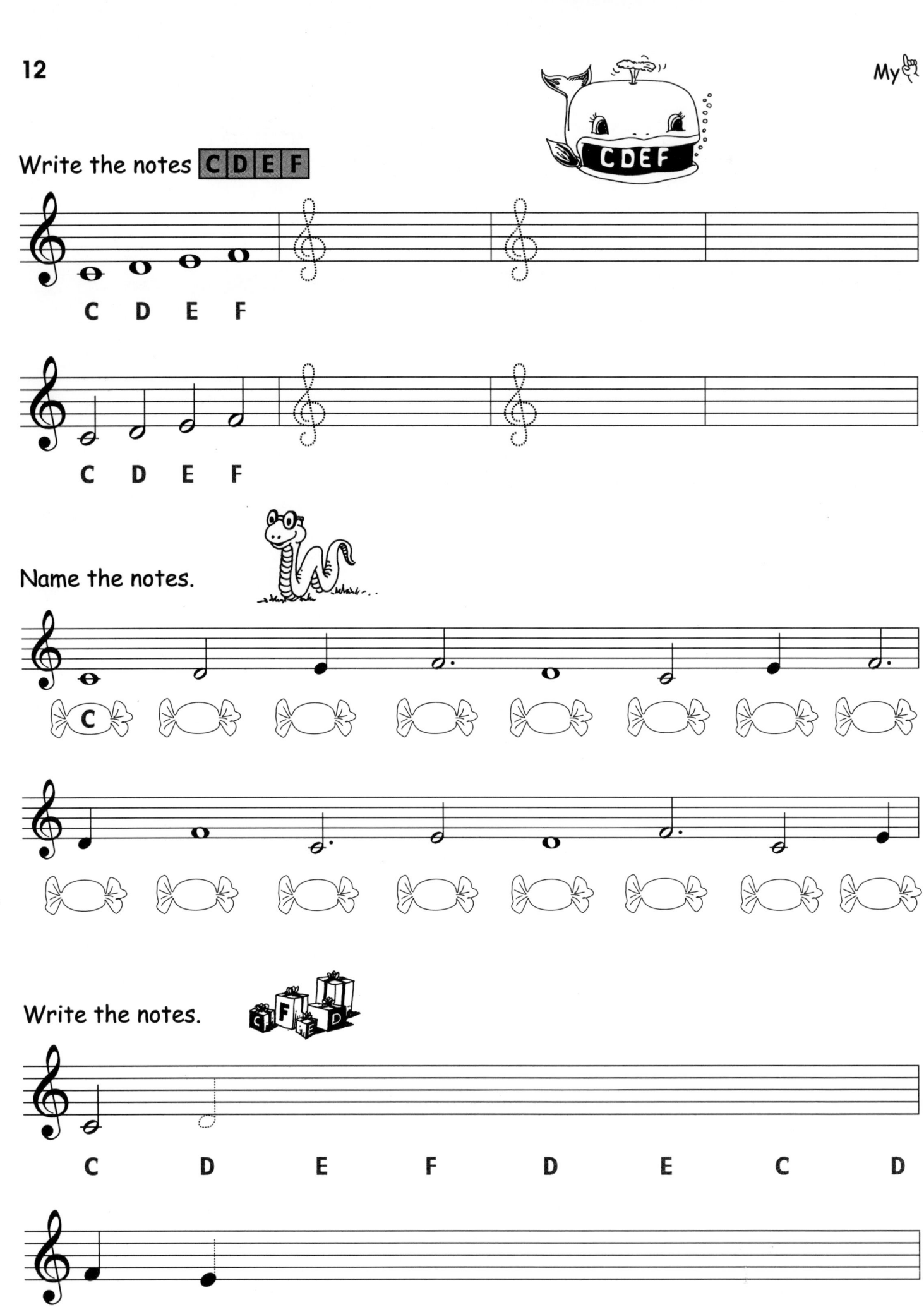

14

GOING CARROTS

Study the picture below and answer the questions.

Which rabbit will find the carrots?   Rabbit _____

Which rabbit will be bitten by the snake?   Rabbit _____

Which 2 rabbits will meet?   Rabbit _____ & Rabbit _____

My ☝

Colour on the keyboard the notes you have to play.

1	C E G	5	C E F
2	D F G	6	D E G
3	C D F	7	C D G
4	E F G	8	D E F

NOTES IN THE BASS

Write the notes C B

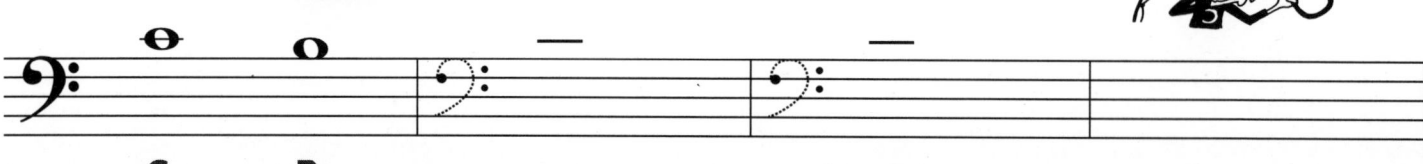

C   B

C   B

Name the notes.

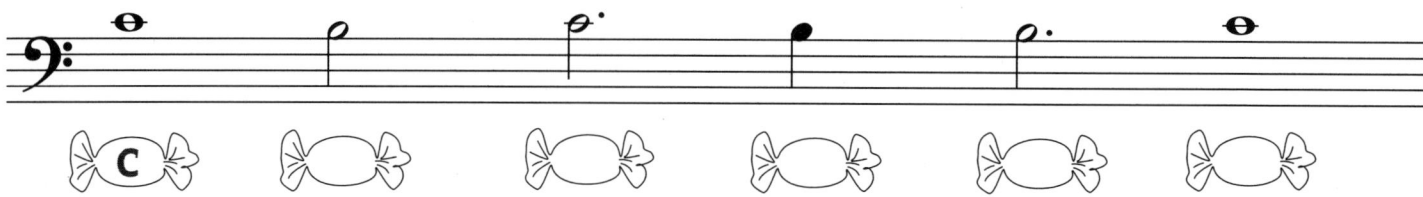

C

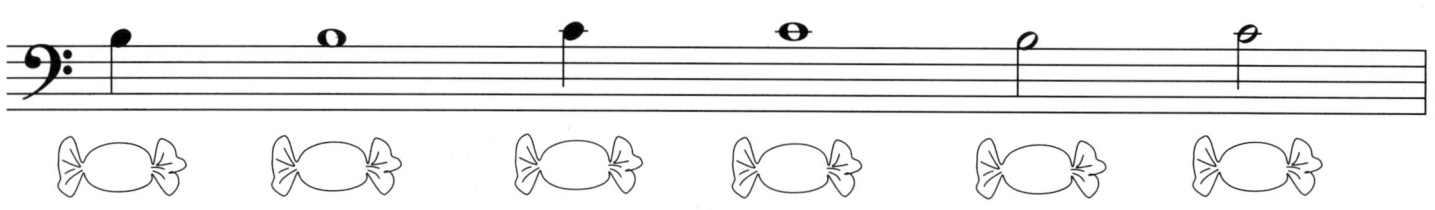

Write the notes.

C   B   B   C   B   C

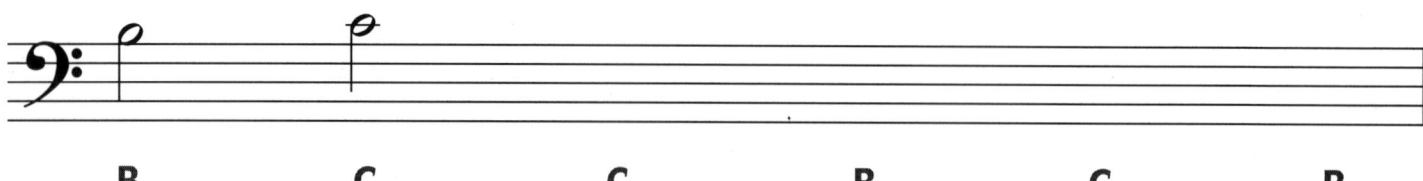

B   C   C   B   C   B

My

17

Write the notes C B A

Name the notes.

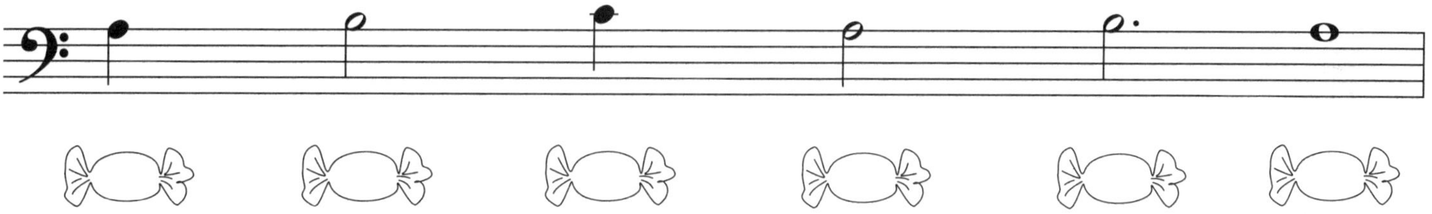

Write the notes.

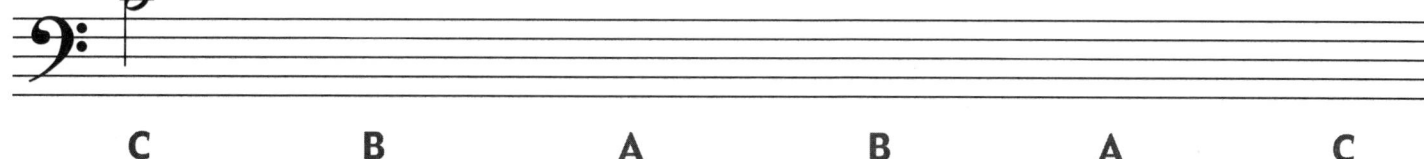

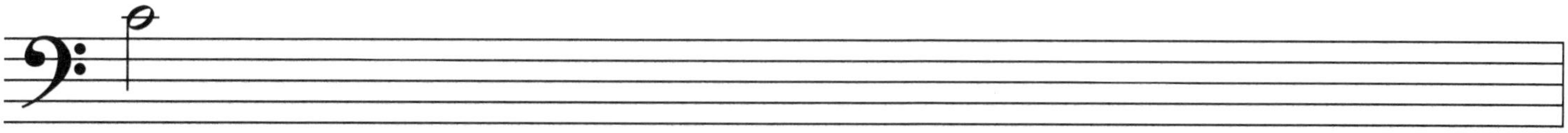

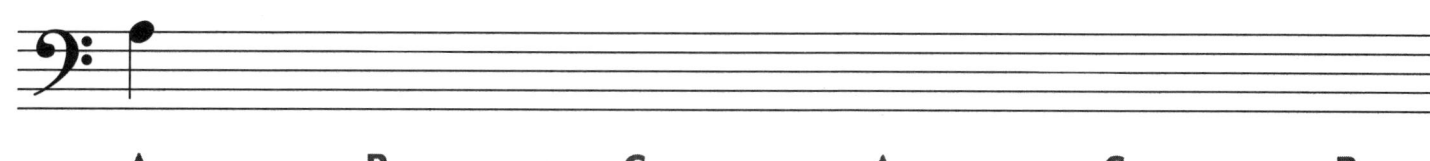

Match the boxes.

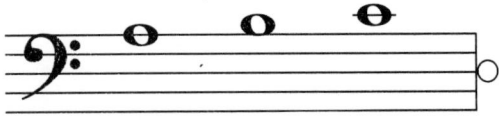

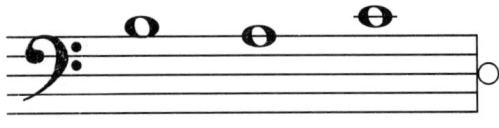

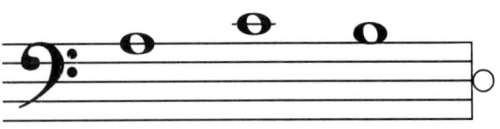

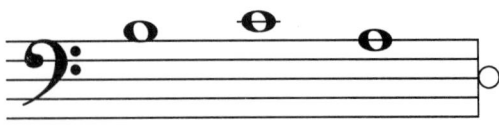

My

Write the notes C B A G

C B A G

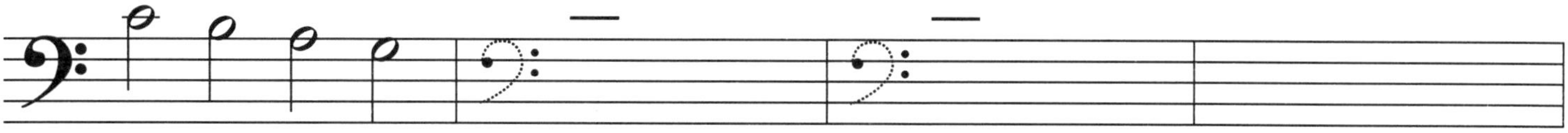

C B A G

Name the notes.

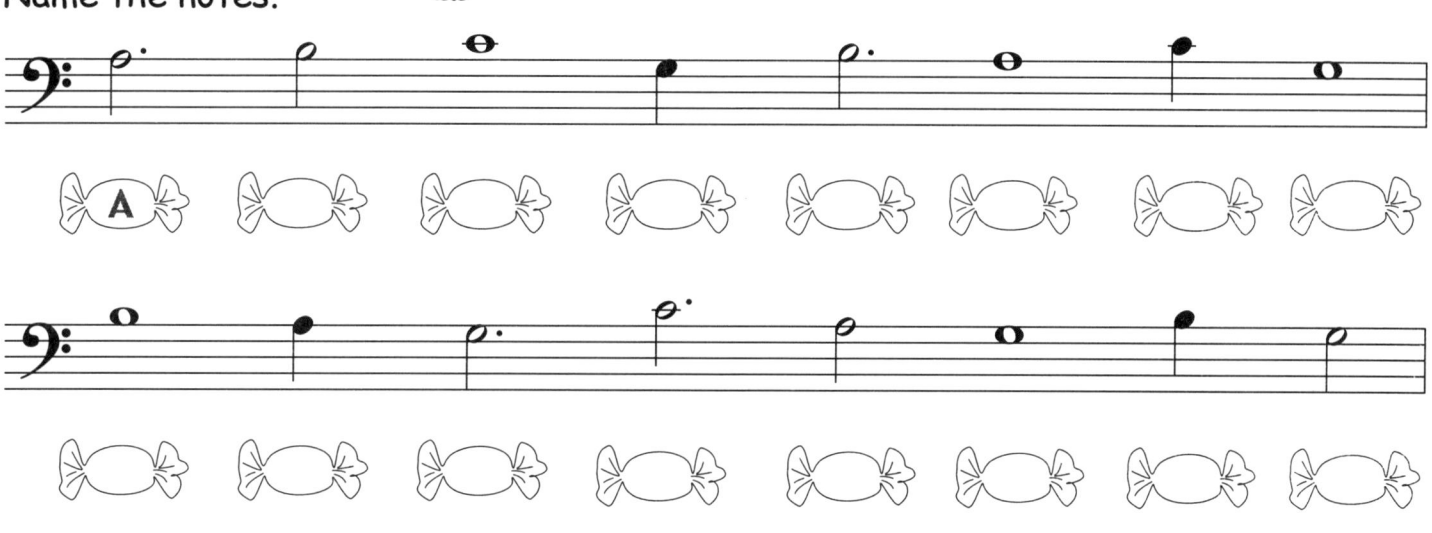

Write the notes.

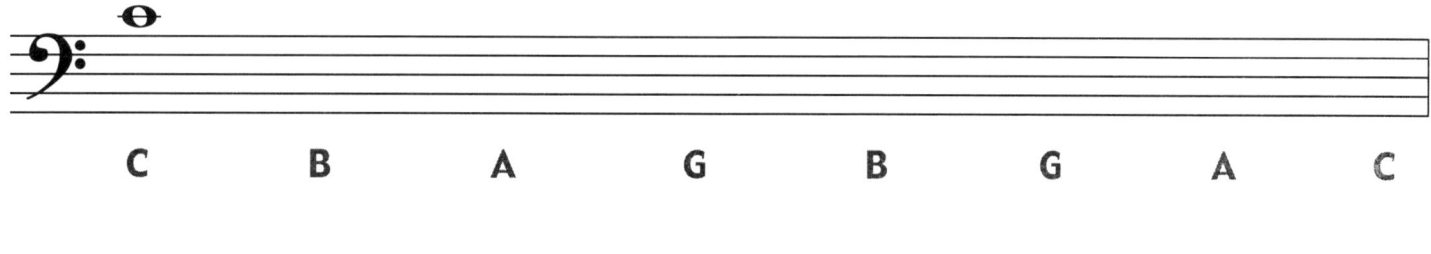

C B A G B G A C

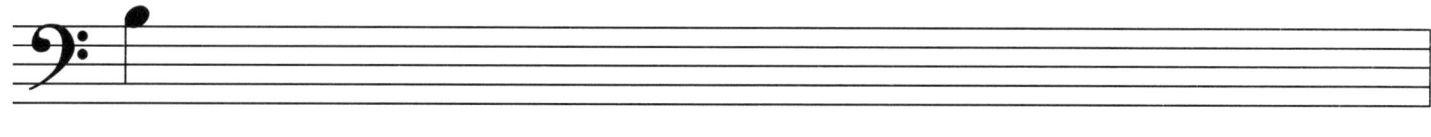

B C G A B C G A

20

Write the notes **C B A G F**

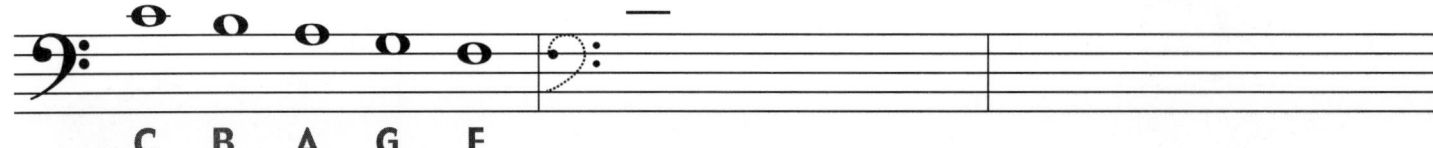

C B A G F

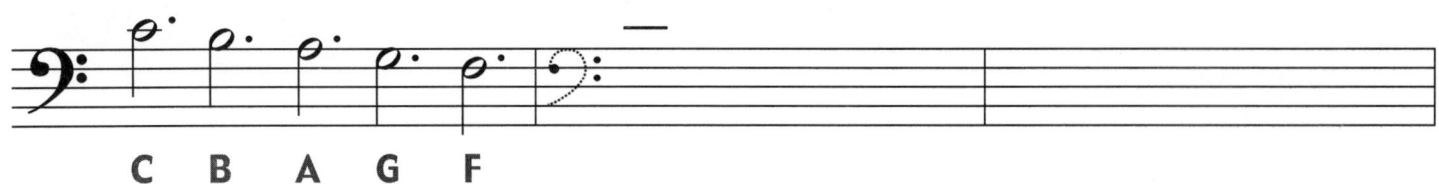

C B A G F

Name the notes.

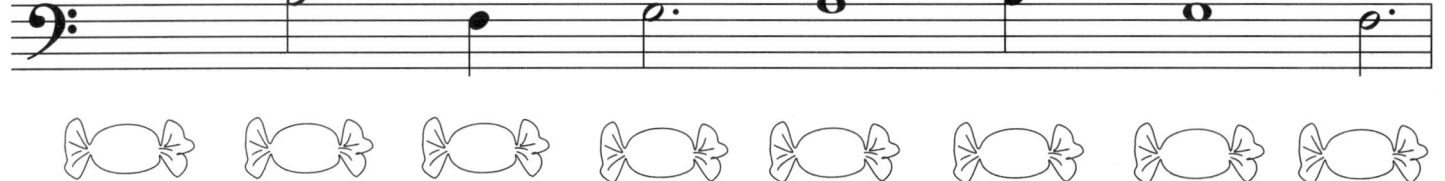

Write the notes.

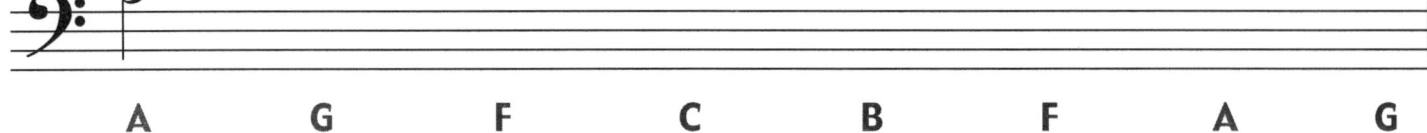

A G F C B F A G

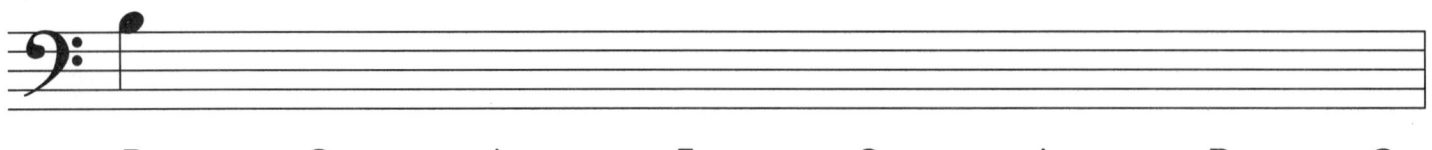

B C A F G A B C

My

Match the notes to the alphabets.

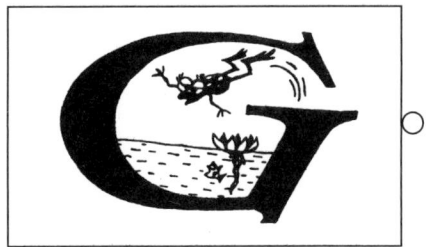

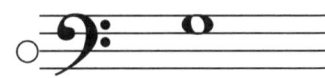

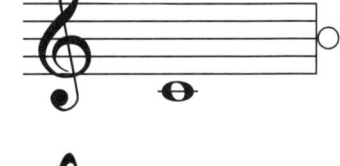
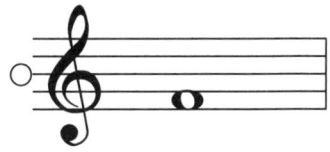

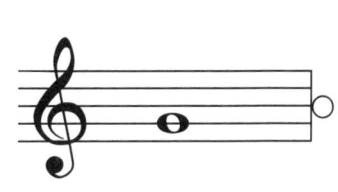

22

Form the words and match to the pictures.

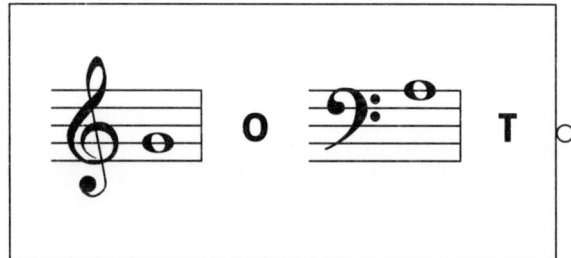 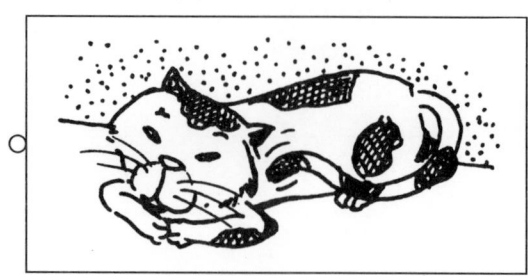

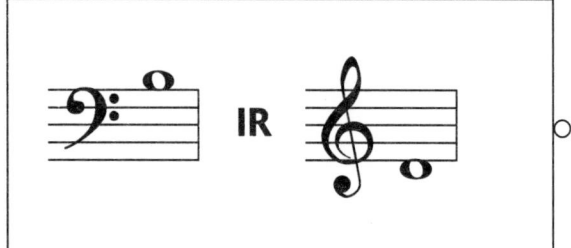 

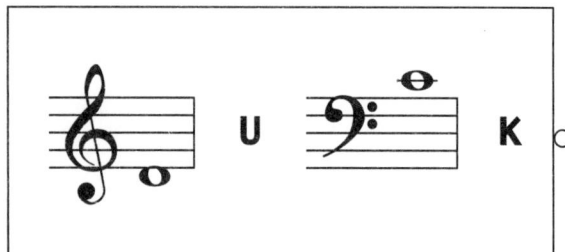 

My

Copy the rests and number of counts.

Semibreve

Counts: 4   4

Minim

Counts: 2   2

Crotchet

Counts: 1   1

Write the number of counts.

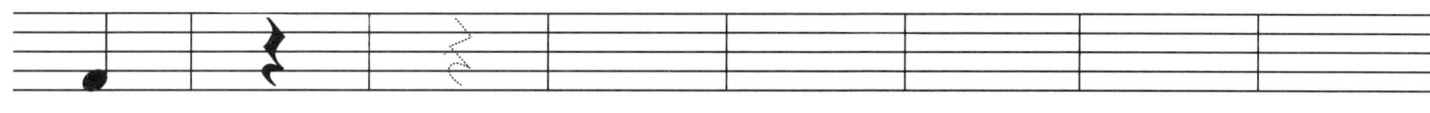

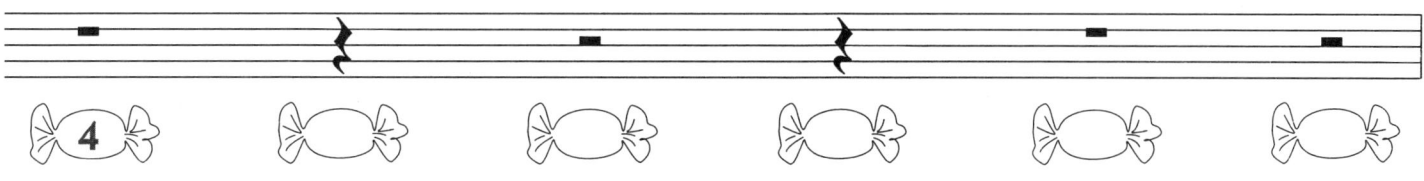

Copy the following.

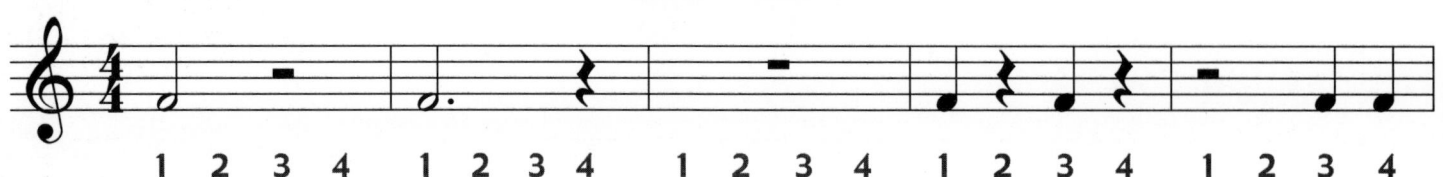

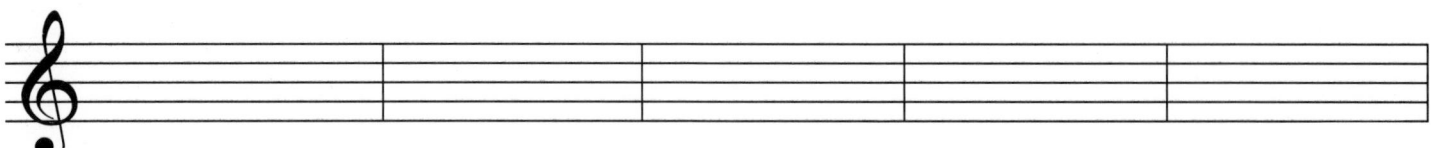

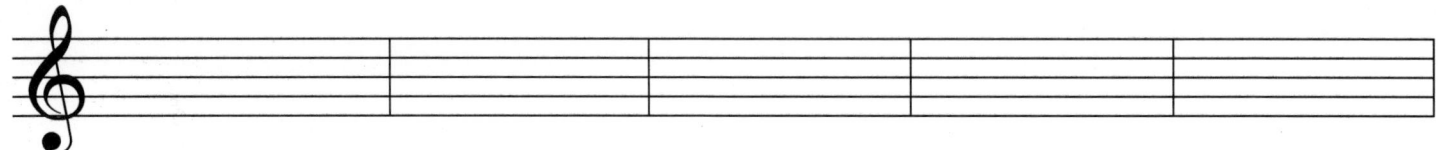

Copy the following.

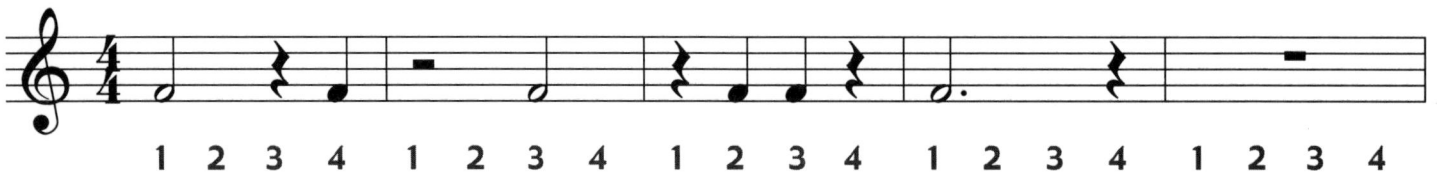

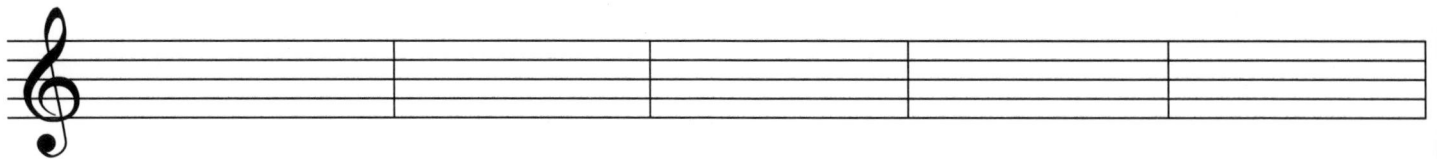

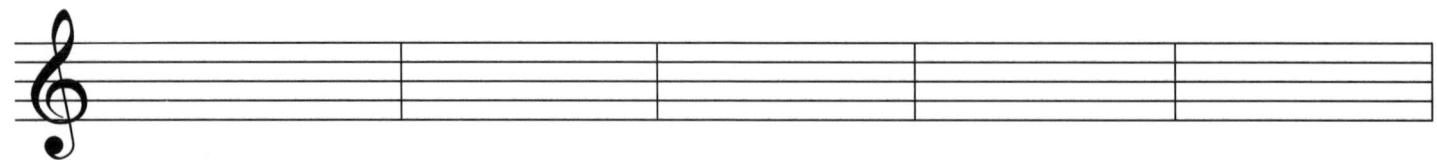

My

25

FIND THE PARTNERS

Help the boys find their partners.
Colour the clothing according to the time-values.
Has everyone found a partner? _____

COUNTS	COLOUR
1	RED
2	BLUE
3	YELLOW
4	GREEN

26

Write the counts in these measures.

1   2   3   4

My 27

Put in bar-lines.

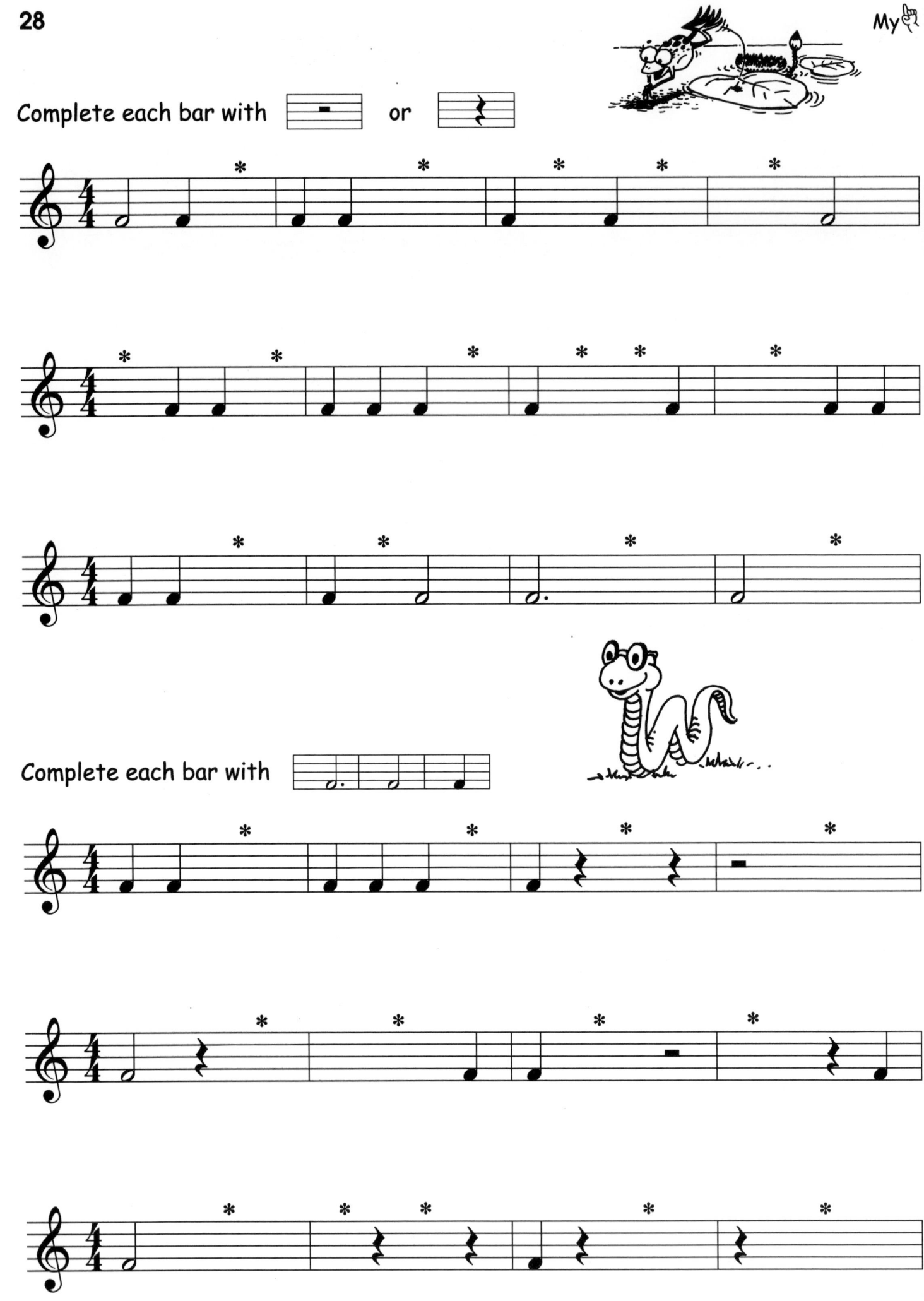

ACCIDENTALS

#	sharp	=	raises a note 1 semitone in pitch
♭	flat	=	lowers a note 1 semitone in pitch
♮	natural	=	restores a note to its original pitch

Trace the accidentals.

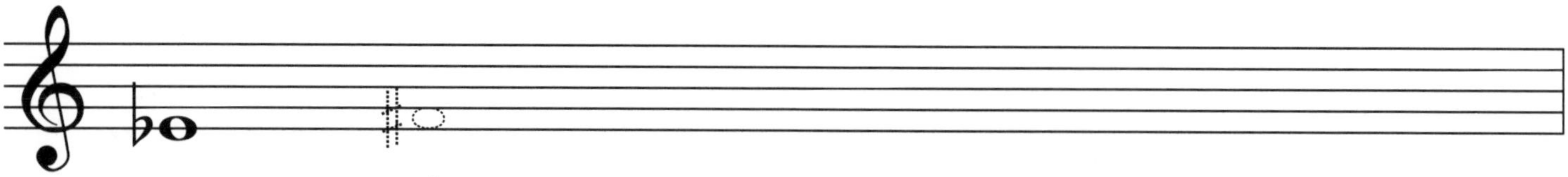

At The Baby-Sitters

1. Write the correct sign (♯, ♭, ♮) on the babies to show family connection.
2. Put your finger at ✻ and trace the route.
3. After work, Mimi, Lili and Lulu went to fetch their children.
   They fetched Mimi's baby, then Lili's and Lulu's.

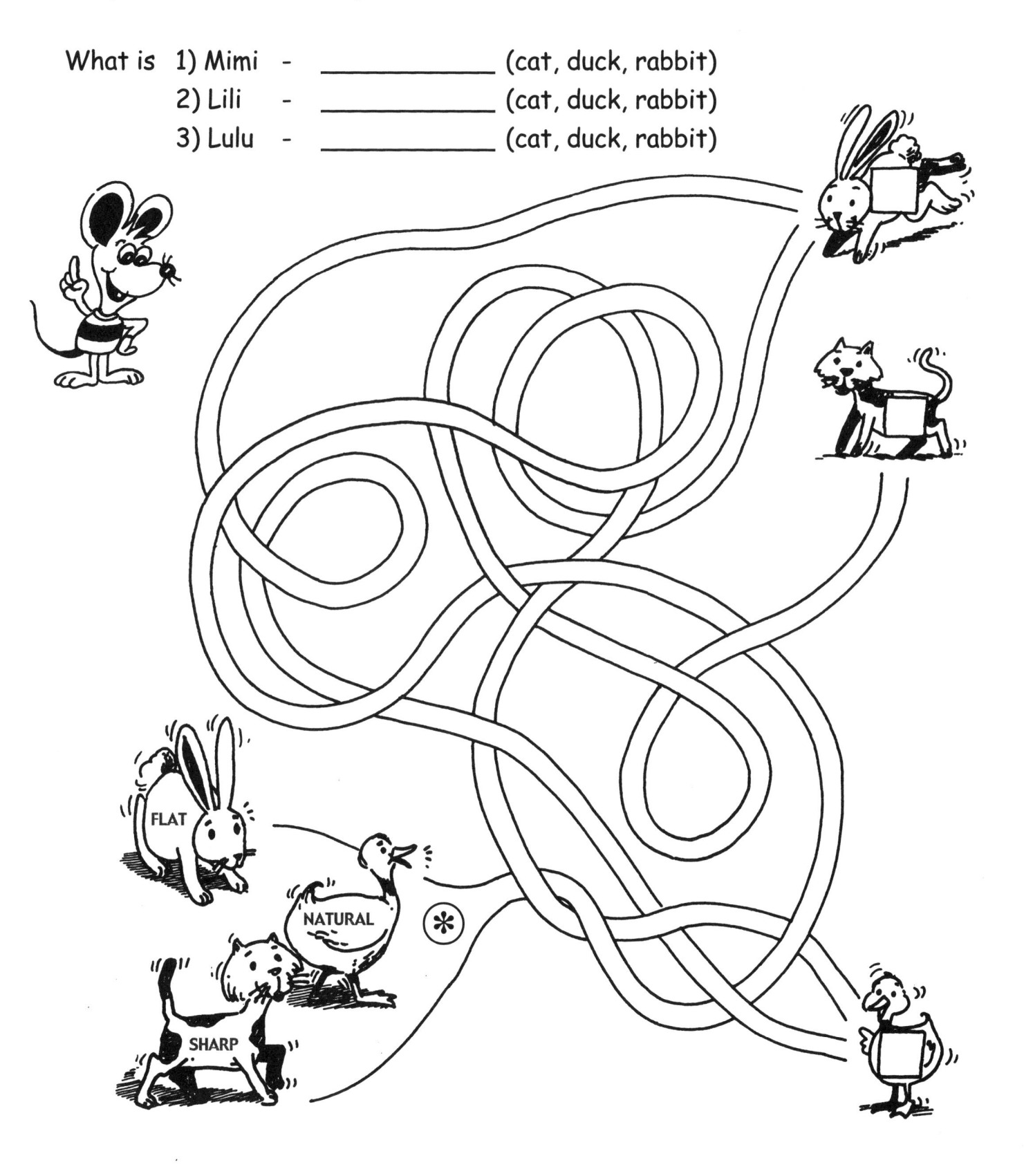

   What is 1) Mimi - _____ (cat, duck, rabbit)
            2) Lili - _____ (cat, duck, rabbit)
            3) Lulu - _____ (cat, duck, rabbit)

32

Name the notes.

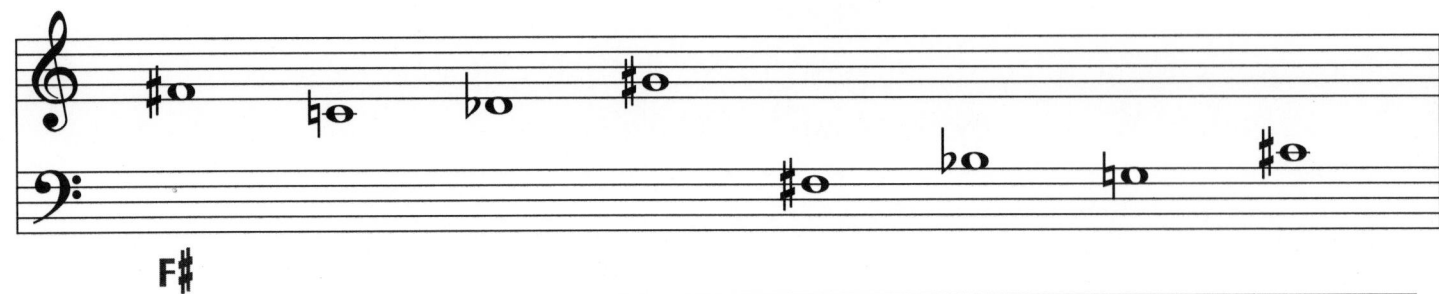

F#

To which note does the sign belong?

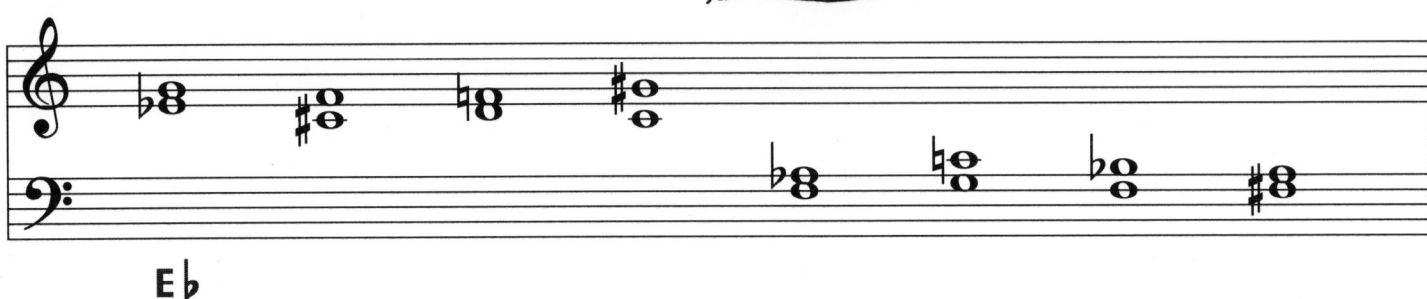

Eb

Prefix the accidental against the note stated.

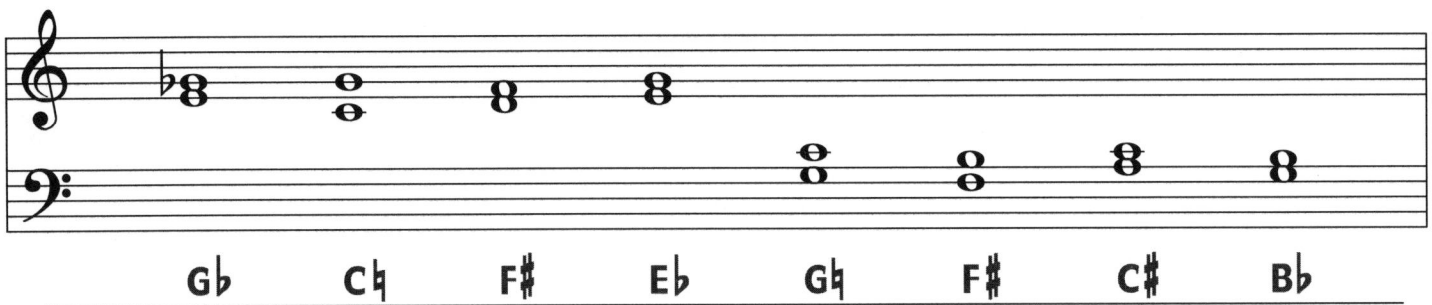

Gb　　Ch　　F#　　Eb　　Gh　　F#　　C#　　Bb

To which note does the sign belong?

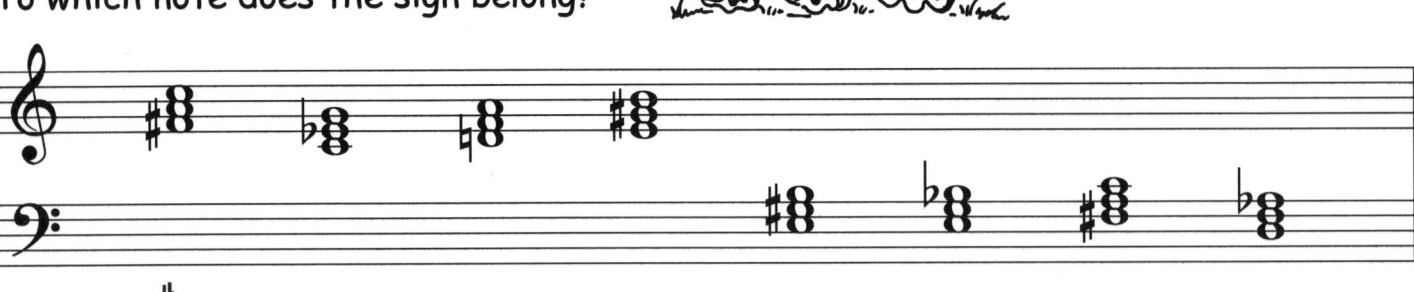

F#

My

POSITION OF STEMS

33

The stems indicate either P or d Pond

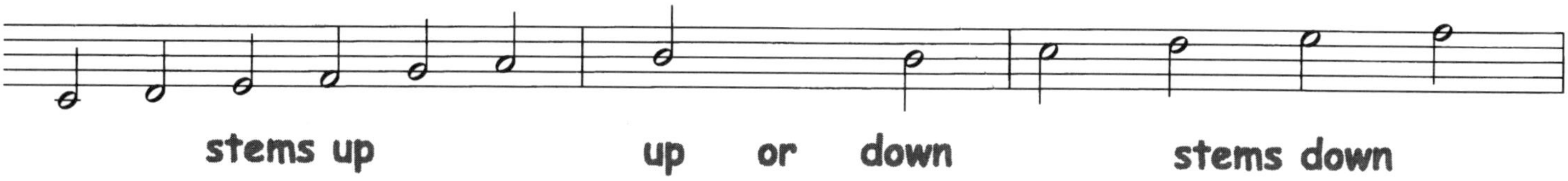

stems up   up   or   down   stems down

Add a stem to every note.

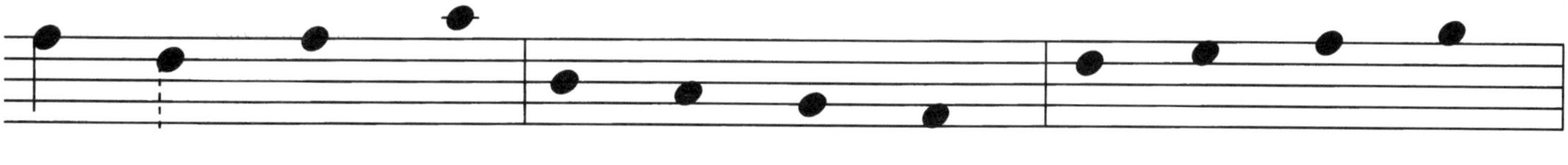

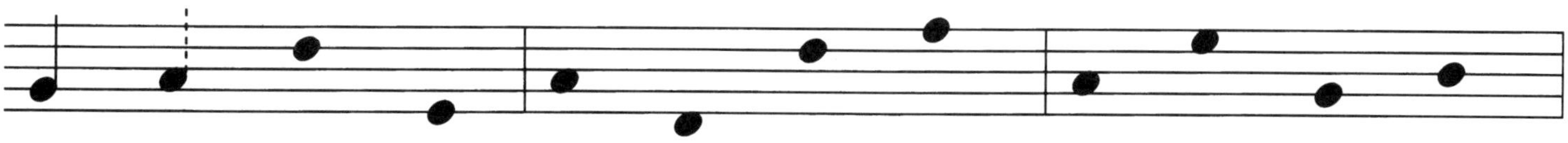

My 👆

TIME SIGNATURES

Write the counts and then the time signatures. $\frac{2}{4}$ $\frac{3}{4}$ $\frac{4}{4}$

1   2

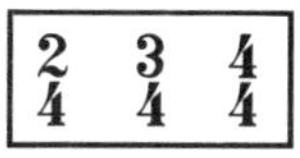

FISHING

These animals are fishing by the river.
Have they caught the correct fish?
Mark (✓) or (✗) on their caps.

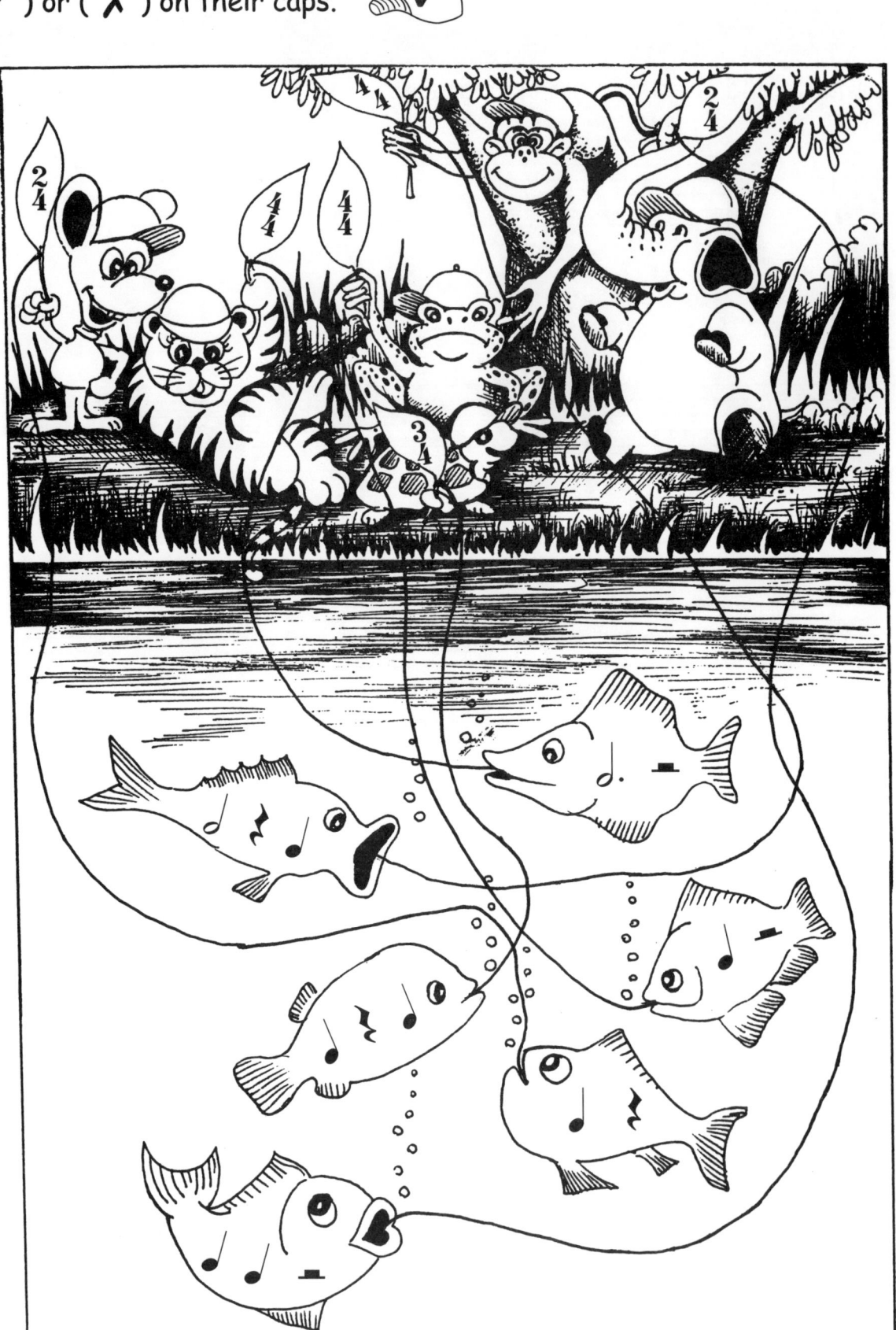

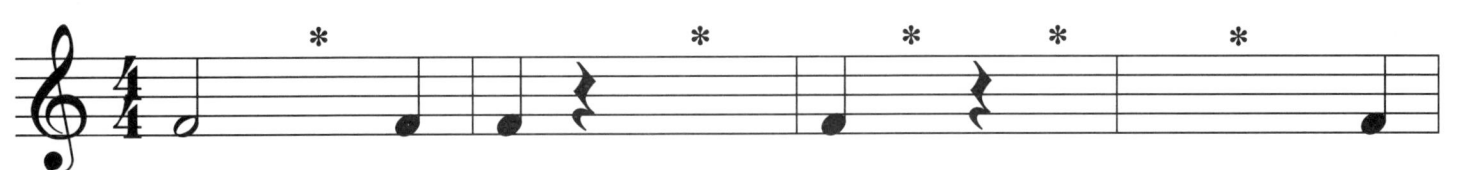

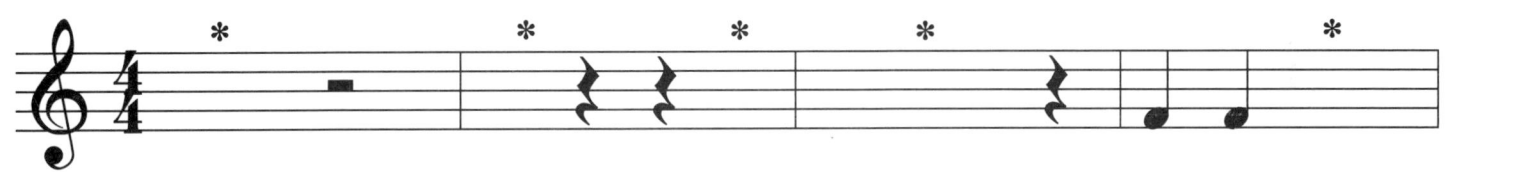

COMPLETE BARS WITH NOTES

37

Complete each bar with ♩ 𝅗𝅥 𝅗𝅥.

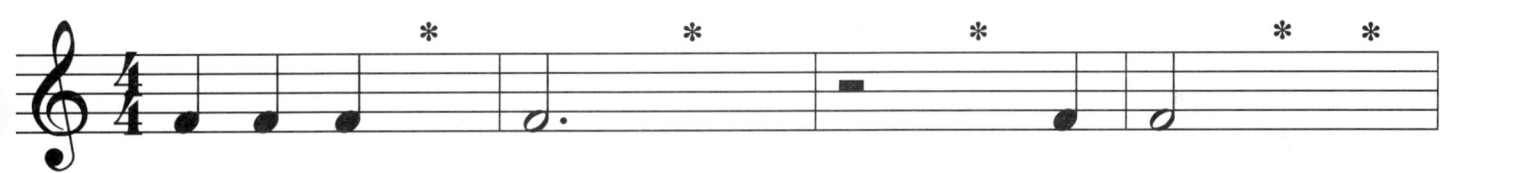

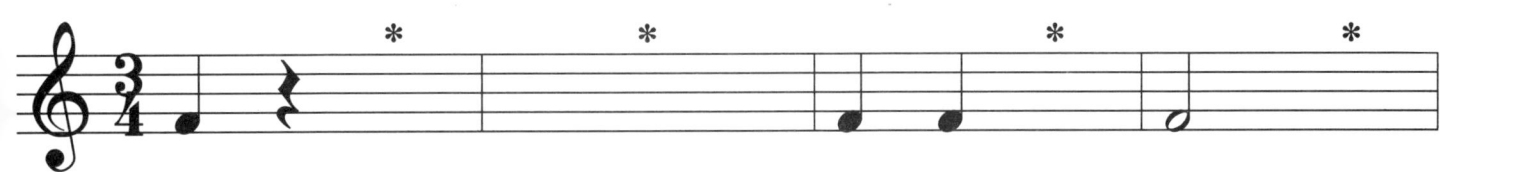

COMPLETE BARS WITH RESTS

A bar rest is used to fill an empty bar of 2/4, 3/4, 4/4 time.

Complete each bar with 𝄽 ― ―

My ☞ **TesT** 39

TOTAL MARKS
100

NAME: _____   DATE: _____

20

1. Name the notes.

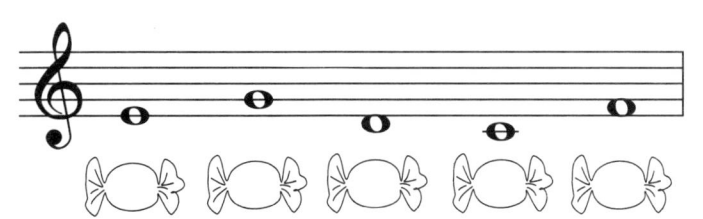

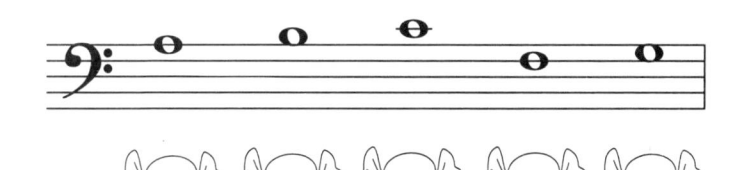

2. Write the number of counts.

10

3. Complete each bar with notes or rests.   o d.   or   ⁊ ▬

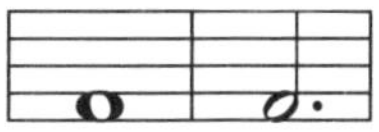

20

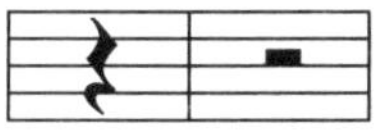

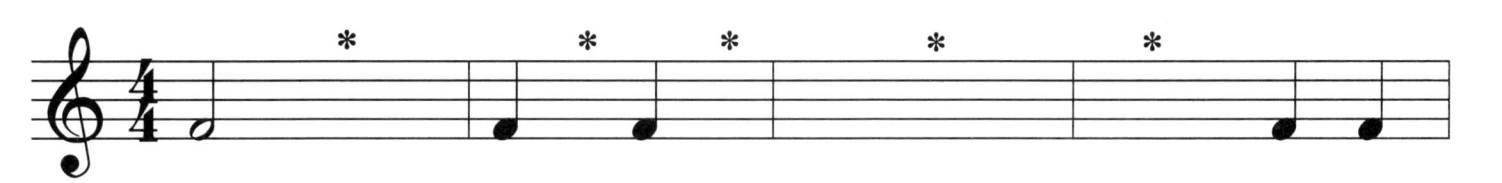

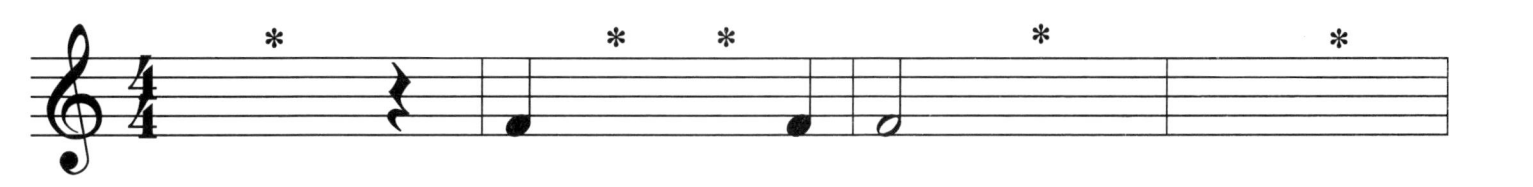

40

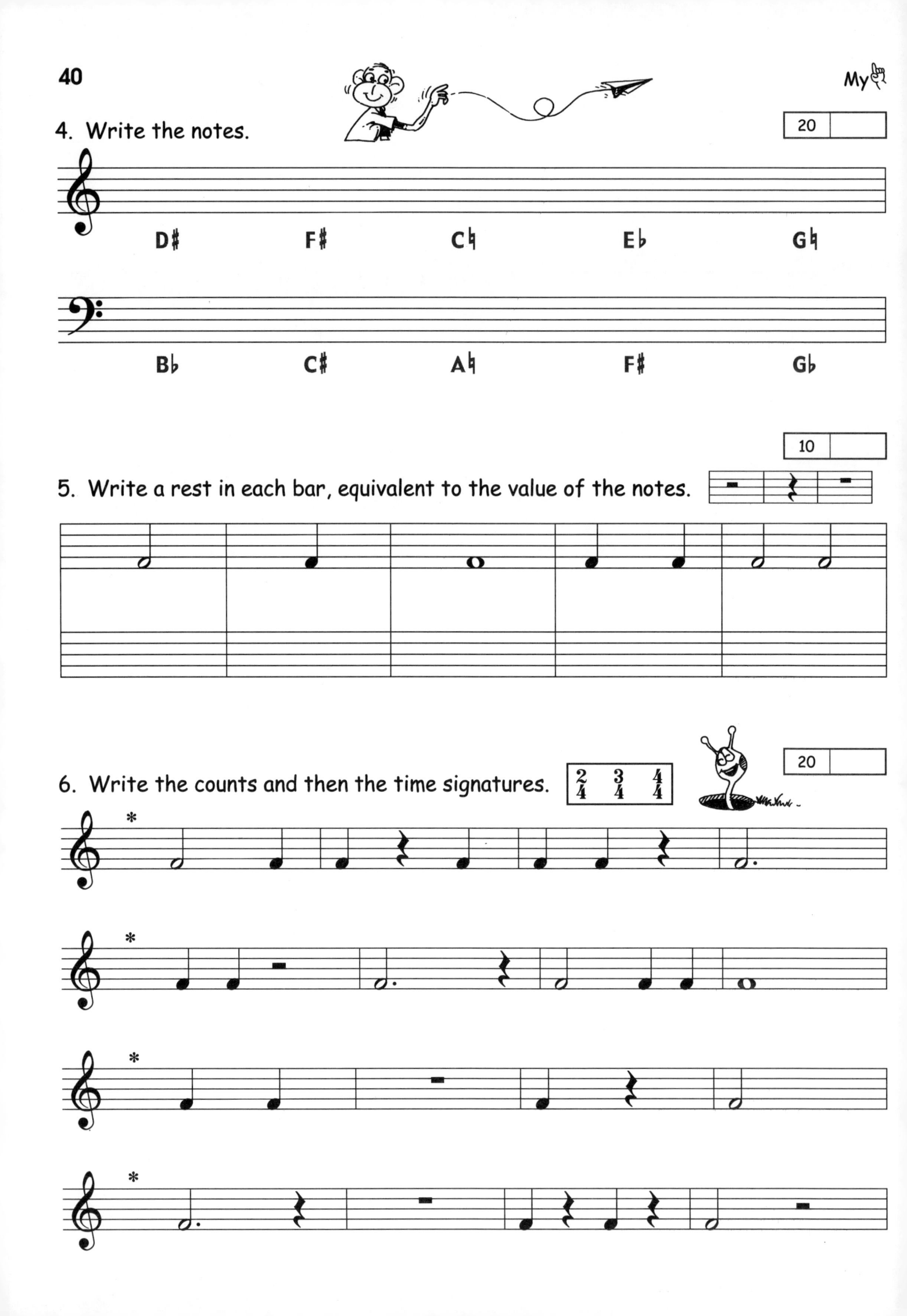

4. Write the notes.

D♯ F♯ C♮ E♭ G♮

B♭ C♯ A♮ F♯ G♭

5. Write a rest in each bar, equivalent to the value of the notes.

6. Write the counts and then the time signatures.

COMPOSING MADE EASY

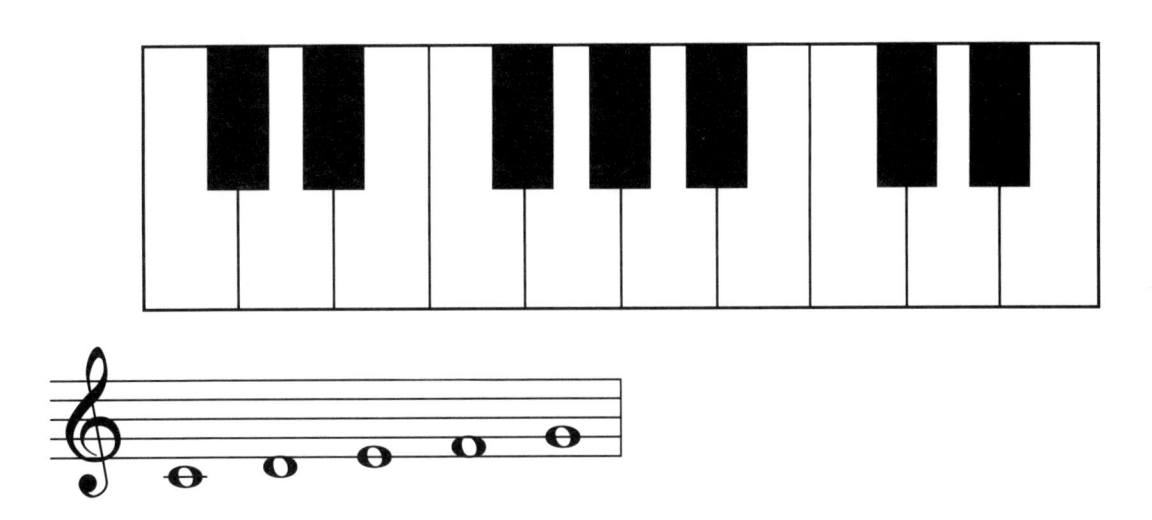

Play every melodic phrase on the keyboard.

Fill in a note where you see this symbol * to complete the melody.

42

Complete the following phrases by adding a note where you see this symbol *

Play every phrase on the keyboard to decide the best note to use.

My ☝

43

Fill the empty bar with notes to complete the phrase.

Notes to use are: middle C D E F G

My

My